A souvenir guide

Felbrigg Hall, Gardens and Estate

Norfolk

Oliver Garnett

National Trust

A Welcoming Home with Wide Horizons

'I have never stayed in any other house where there was such an atmosphere of peace and serenity.'
Brinsley Ford, who visited Felbrigg in the 1950s

As you come up the drive through Felbrigg's open parkland, you instinctively relax. For this is a welcoming place of beauty and tranquillity.

Today, we can best see Felbrigg through the eyes of its last squire, Robert Wyndham Ketton-Cremer. A distinguished historian of Norfolk, he loved his books and his trees, but his greatest interest was in the people of Felbrigg, past and present. His book, *Felbrigg: The Story of a House*, has become a classic, bringing to life the stories of those who have lived and worked here over the centuries. And what stories they are! Of perilous exploration of an Alpine glacier and of a firework explosion; of a scandalous Victorian court case and bankruptcy. Through all the ups and downs, Felbrigg's owners have remained stubbornly devoted to the house and the estate, so that,

miraculously, it still preserves its historic collections and the surrounding landscape.

The cry of the plover is still, if rarely, heard overhead, as big Norfolk skies frame perfect sunsets. The ancient woodland shelters the estate from the biting north winds. The open pasture land and lake are a haven for plants and wildlife. The Walled Garden and orchard are dominated by the working dove-house.

The woodland 'Victory V' – a personal war memorial created by the last squire to remember his beloved brother Dick, who was killed in Crete in 1941 – reminds us how the people of Felbrigg continue to shape the place.

The people of Felbrigg

1621–4: The south front is built for **Thomas Windham** and his father **Sir John** in Jacobean style.

1680s: Thomas's son, **William Windham I** (1), extends the Jacobean house with the new red-brick west wing, employing the gentleman-architect William Samwell as his designer.

Early 18th century: William Windham I's son, **Ashe Windham** (2), who had succeeded in 1689, builds a new service courtyard on the east side of the house and the Orangery. He also completes the interior of the west wing.

1749–61: **William Windham II** (3) had returned from an extensive Grand Tour of Europe in 1742, weighed down with books and pictures. On his father Ashe's death in 1749, William engages the architect James Paine to refashion the interiors to display his new possessions. Paine's Rococo rooms are among the most pleasing of their period.

Early 19th century: William Windham II's son, **William Windham III** (4), becomes a leading politician, but does little to Felbrigg. He dies in 1810, leaving the estate to his nephew **Vice-Admiral William Lukin** (5), on condition that he changes his name to Windham. In 1824 the Admiral employs the architect W.J. Donthorn to remodel Ashe Windham's service wing and to build a neo-Tudor stable block.

1840s: The Admiral's son **William Howe Windham** (6) alters the Great Hall – the last significant architectural change at Felbrigg.

1854–1923: Felbrigg declines rapidly during the brief lifetime of the eccentric spendthrift '**Mad Windham**' (7). The estate is sold to **John Ketton** in 1863. In the early 20th century there is a period of unchecked decay. Despite this, the house and its contents survive.

1923–69: The Cremer family, to whom the estate passed in 1923, on condition that they take the name of Ketton, gradually repairs the run-down house. The last squire of Felbrigg, the scholar **Robert Wyndham Ketton-Cremer** (8), devotedly carries on this work. On his death in 1969, he leaves the house, gardens and estate to the National Trust.

Felbrigg and its People

Felbrigg lies a mile or so from the north coast of Norfolk among woods grown over heathland on what counts for a hill in the county.

The Felbriggs of Felbrigg

When the Domesday Book survey was made in 1086, Felbrigg belonged to the Bigod family, who were immensely powerful earls of Norfolk. It then passed to a family that took its name from the place. Remarkably, we know what the 14th- and 15th-century de Felbriggs looked like, thanks to a magnificent series of memorial brasses in St Margaret's church, which stands in the south-east corner of the park. (The brasses were conserved in 1987, having suffered from centuries of corrosion by bat urine.)

Simon de Felbrigg (d.1351) and his wife Alice de Thorpe are shown in modest civilian dress. By contrast, Simon's son, Roger de Felbrigg (d. c.1380), wears full armour, and his wife Elizabeth has an elaborate headdress. Roger fought the French in the campaigns of the 1350s (the first of many owners of Felbrigg to venture abroad). He died in faraway Prussia.

Right St Margaret's church, Felbrigg, was probably rebuilt by Sir Simon Felbrigg in the early 15th century

A Brass in Felbrigg Church Norfolk.

Drawn Etched & Published by J.S. Cotman Jan.y 1815.

Left A tomb brass in the church commemorates (from left to right) Simon de Felbrigg, his wife Alice, his son Roger, and daughter-in-law, Elizabeth

Below Sir Simon Felbrigg and his first wife Margaret (d.1416) from an etching by J.S. Cotman

The King's knight

With Roger's son, Sir Simon Felbrigg (d.1442), the family reached the peak of its power and wealth, at the court of Richard II. In 1395 he was made royal standard bearer; he was also knighted and awarded the Order of the Garter. His first wife was Margaret of Teschen (Silesia, in today's Czech Republic), maid-of-honour to the Queen, Anne of Bohemia, wife of Richard II. But all this royal favour came to a sudden end in 1399 with the overthrow of Richard by the Lancastrian rebels. Sir Simon survived the coup, and when he came to commission a tomb brass for his late wife in 1416, he defiantly decorated it with the symbols of his lost power: knightly armour, royal standard, Garter ribbon and Yorkist fetterlock (padlock) emblem. Similarly, when Sir Simon rebuilt the church at Felbrigg, the lion rampant and fetterlock (an equine shackle) from his coat of arms featured prominently. Very little of the Felbriggs' medieval house survives, bar some masonry and brickwork in the cellars.

The Wyndhams

Sir Simon had no sons and so on his death in 1442 he instructed that the estate should be sold. The buyer was John Wyndham, a thoroughly unsavoury character who was very unpopular with the locals. He only became absolute owner on the death of Sir Simon's second wife in 1461, but his right to the property was still being challenged by the Felbrigg family. Sir John Felbrigg broke into the house while Wyndham was away and dragged the latter's wife out by her hair. A furious John Wyndham 'saeth that he will have Felbrigg again ere Michaelmas, or there shall be five hundred heads broke therefor'. Ultimately it was cash, not violence, that persuaded Sir John Felbrigg to leave. Wyndham died in full possession in 1475.

Death on the scaffold

John Wyndham's son, another John, married into the Howard family, powerful dukes of Norfolk. He survived the fall of Richard III; indeed, he was knighted by Henry VII for his service at the battle of Stoke in Nottinghamshire in 1487. However, his luck ran out in the reign of Henry VII, when he was implicated in the de la Pole conspiracy to overthrow the king. He was beheaded on Tower Hill on 6 May 1502. Beside him on the scaffold that day was James Tyrrell, prime suspect for the murder of the Princes in the Tower.

Sir Thomas Wyndham (d.1522), warrior mariner

With the support of his Howard cousins (two of whom became Lord High Admiral), Sir John's son, Thomas, enjoyed a very successful naval career. Indeed, in 1512 he captained the most

Above A junior branch of the Wyndham family lived at Orchard Wyndham in Somerset. This early 18th-century English School oil painting depicts the estate with the town and harbour of Watchet in the distance. The pier was built by Sir William Wyndham, 3rd Bt. In the foreground are a terrace and figures with an avenue beyond leading to a fountain and stables. The house is to the right

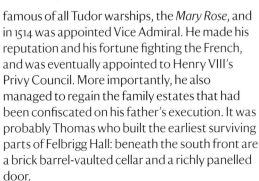

Below Sir Thomas Wyndham became captain of the most famous Tudor ship, the *Mary Rose*. Built in Portsmouth in 1509–10, the carrack warship was one of the first to be able to fire a full broadside of cannons. She was thought to be named after King Henry VIII's sister Mary and the rose, the Tudor emblem. The ship is depicted in a modern painting by Richard Willis (1924–)

Sir Thomas's grandson Roger Windham inherited in 1569 and over the next three decades wasted his fortune in numerous fruitless law suits. To pay the legal bills, he was forced to mortgage much of the estate to his wealthy cousin, Sir John Wyndham of Orchard Wyndham in Somerset. Roger's only achievement was to change the Norfolk branch of the family name from Wyndham to Windham.

In 1599 Roger's youngest brother Thomas was left to pick up the pieces, which he did. He died childless within the year, but in that time had established the Somerset Wyndhams as unquestioned heirs to Felbrigg. In gratitude for Thomas's generosity, Sir John set up a grand memorial brass to his cousin in Felbrigg church.

The new century was to bring dramatic change.

famous of all Tudor warships, the *Mary Rose*, and in 1514 was appointed Vice Admiral. He made his reputation and his fortune fighting the French, and was eventually appointed to Henry VIII's Privy Council. More importantly, he also managed to regain the family estates that had been confiscated on his father's execution. It was probably Thomas who built the earliest surviving parts of Felbrigg Hall: beneath the south front are a brick barrel-vaulted cellar and a richly panelled door.

Building the Jacobean house

Sir John Wyndham (1558–1645) and

Thomas Windham (1585–1654)

To save money, Jane Coningsby (who had kept house for her bachelor brother Thomas Windham) was allowed to remain in residence until her death in 1608. The following year Sir John Wyndham made the long journey from Somerset to Felbrigg for the first, and perhaps the only, time. He was welcomed with lavish quantities of claret, pork, lamb, chicken, venison and eels by tenants and neighbours, naturally anxious to know his plans for Felbrigg. Running the estate from Somerset was impractical, and so he settled on his second son, Thomas, a young London lawyer, to re-found the Norfolk branch of the family. To establish the new line, in 1620 Thomas married Elizabeth Lytton of Knebworth, and began building a new home on the site of the

Tudor house. All seemed set fair when Elizabeth produced the hoped-for son and heir, John, two years later, but, tragically, she died in childbirth. Undaunted, Thomas ploughed on with the project. His architect is not known, but was almost certainly Robert Lyminge, who was working at nearby Blickling at the same time and in the same style. Many of the same craftsmen were also employed, including the plasterer Edward Stanyon.

The new house

What survives today of the Jacobean house is largely the south front. In the style of the period, it combines external symmetry and large windows with an asymmetrical medieval arrangement inside: a central screens passage separated the Great Hall from the service quarters, and a long gallery ran the length of the attic above. In a county short of good building stone, the core of the building was brick, covered in render in imitation of more expensive stone. Stone was restricted to the window frames, parapet and classical door surround. Work was completed by 1624, when Smith the mason was paid for carving two lions to stand on the east and west gables.

Above The coats of arms of Sir John and Thomas above the entrance door celebrate the re-establishment of the Windham family at Felbrigg and proclaim it as a joint enterprise between father and son

Opposite The south front of the Jacobean house

War and peace

When the Civil War broke out in 1642, Thomas sided with Parliament, like most of the Norfolk gentry. He came through the war unscathed, unlike his Somerset cousins, whose loyalties were agonisingly divided. After two decades living in his grand new house as a widower, Thomas remarried in about 1644 Elizabeth Mede, who bore him a second son, William.

Thomas's elder son John, who inherited Felbrigg in 1654, saw no need to make changes to the house, which was then only 30 years old. Sadly, his efforts to produce an heir were fruitless, despite marrying four times. He died in 1665, aged only 43. He was succeeded by his young half-brother William, whose coming of age in 1668 ushered in a splendid new era for Felbrigg.

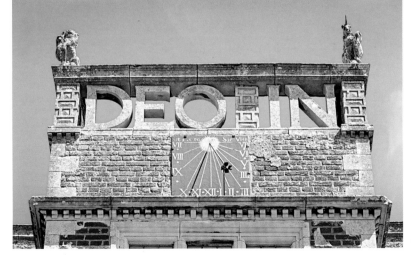

Left The parapet features a religious text appropriate for the highest point on the building: 'GLORIA DEO IN EXCELSIS' ('Glory to God in the Highest')

A grand house made grander

William I (1647–89) and Katherine (1652–1729) Windham

'Gay, generous, warm-hearted, a devoted wife, a loving but thoroughly sensible mother to a large family of children'

R.W. Ketton-Cremer on Katherine Windham

Far left **William Windham I**, who built the west wing; painted by Sir Peter Lely (Dining Room)

Left **Katherine Windham**, who ran the Felbrigg estate after her husband's death; painted by Sir Peter Lely and studio (Dining Room)

In 1669, a year after he came of age, William married Katherine Ashe, the daughter of a rich Twickenham merchant who had helped to finance the Royalist cause during the Civil War. Her portrait shows her picking orange blossom, the symbol of marriage. It was, by all accounts, a close and loving marriage, and she emerges from the family papers as a very attractive character.

'An excellent architect, that has built severall delicate houses.'

The antiquary John Aubrey on the architect William Samwell

Improving the house

By the 1670s Felbrigg was beginning to look old-fashioned and too small for the Windhams' growing family (eight of their eleven offspring survived childhood). So William called in the gentleman-architect William Samwell. Samwell's first plan, dated August 1674, was very ambitious, envisaging three new wings around an enclosed central courtyard. Windham rejected this scheme: 'I thought his first design too bigg & not convenient.' A more modest version was produced in February 1675. After further tinkering, they finally settled on the design as built. This comprised a new west wing, physically

Opposite above **William Samwell's design for the west front**

Opposite below **The west (left) and south (right) fronts**

He devoted much of his energies to his woods, and was an assiduous reader of John Evelyn's *Sylva*, the leading work of the period on tree-planting. This was seen as the patriotic duty of landowners, as timber was vital for the expanding Royal Navy. His favourite species was sweet chestnut, which grows well at Felbrigg, but he planted much else. In 1676 he recorded, 'I did then plant 4000 Oakes, 800 Ashes, 600 Birches, 70 Beeches, and 50 Crabs, which were all small.' His friends tried to interest him in politics, but without success: 'I confess I take soe much delight in my Nursery and Garden that I don't envye the Knight [Sir John Hobart of Blickling] the honour of being in the house [of Commons].' William died at the age of only 42, leaving a grief-stricken widow and a sixteen-year-old heir, Ashe.

and stylistically separated from the Jacobean south front. It was built from handsome red brick and relies for its presence on a sophisticated sense of proportion. Work proceeded slowly, and was not finished until about 1686, by which date Samwell had been dead for ten years. Most of Samwell's interiors have gone, but the magnificent plasterwork ceilings in the Drawing Room and the Cabinet still survive. These were probably the work of the master plasterer Edward Goudge, who was creating similar ceilings at Belton in Lincolnshire (also NT).

A patriotic and unpolitical landowner

Among the family archives are two green vellum-bound ledgers, in which William recorded all his purchases and the details of his estate management. They were intended to be not just a record of his activities, but also a guide for his successors. He managed farms for quite long periods though there were times when he delegated the work to his tenants under the watchful eye of an agent, John Salman. William proved to be an astute and sensible landlord, who was patient with his more wayward tenants.

'My Dear Dear Husband left me the 9th June 1689 having made me Hapy 20 years.'

Katherine Windham records her husband's death

Dangerous times

Ashe Windham (1673–1749)

Katherine Windham outlived her husband by 40 years and continued to oversee the estate until her son Ashe came of age in 1694. He was educated at Eton and King's College, Cambridge, where his near-contemporaries included Robert Walpole (then an obscure neighbouring landowner, but later to be Britain's first Prime Minister). In 1693 he set off on the Grand Tour with his Scottish tutor Patrick St Clair, who was later to oversee the Felbrigg estate in Ashe's absence. Ashe kept a London house in fashionable Soho Square, but maintained a close interest in activities at Felbrigg. One of his first projects was the Orangery, which he may have designed himself. A miniature version of the west wing, the Orangery employed the recent invention of sash-windows. Hundreds of thousands of red bricks were made on site for the Orangery, a new park wall and new service

Left Ashe Windham (1673–1749), who built the Orangery, painted by Sir Godfrey Kneller (Dining Room)

Below Hester Buckworth, Ashe Windham's fiancée, who died of smallpox in 1708, before they could marry; studio of Sir Godfrey Kneller (Stair Hall)

quarters. At the same time Ashe spent large amounts on a smart new livery of blue jackets and red waistcoats for his indoor staff.

Early in 1708 Ashe fell in love with Hester Buckworth, the daughter of a London merchant – much to the disappointment of his mother, who had hoped for a more lucrative match. However, in May the same year Hester died from a sudden attack of smallpox. But within the year Ashe was married to Elizabeth Dobyns. She was a wealthy heiress, but in every other respect the marriage proved to be a disaster. Cracks soon started appearing between Elizabeth and her unhappy husband. An only child, William, was born in 1717, but this only made matters worse, as the couple quarrelled over his education. They finally separated in 1720, and the following year Ashe suffered some kind of nervous breakdown, which obliged him to spend long periods away from Felbrigg, taking the waters at Bath and Bristol.

Ashe made few further changes at Felbrigg in his later years, partly because the family was forced to retrench, having been caught up in the 1720 financial crash nicknamed the 'South Sea Bubble' after the eponymous trading company.

Above The Orangery, seen across the ha-ha, is set in trees at a right angle to the west wing. It may have been designed by Ashe Windham

A man of the world

William Windham II (1717–61)

Left **William Windham II as a young man**, a pastel in the Yellow Bedroom by Barthélémy du Pan, probably drawn in Geneva while on his Grand Tour

Below *View of the Ice Valley* from William Windham's *An Account of the Glaciers or Ice Alps in Savoy*, 1744

In 1723 Benjamin Stillingfleet, from whom the term 'Blue Stocking' originated, was appointed 'Master Billy's' tutor, giving his pupil as good an education as he could have received anywhere in Europe. Windham's studies in classics, maths, science, music and modern languages left him with a fascination for the world. He didn't go to university, but instead set off on a Grand Tour of Europe with Stillingfleet. By February 1739 they were in Florence, and they spent Easter in Rome. Patrick St Clair corresponded with William and encouraged Ashe Windham to increase his son's allowance by £500, 'for no doubt he desires to lay it out on books, and pictures, and perhaps

medals'. The extra money was quickly spent on commissioning a series of views of the historic sites of Rome, on Italian and French paintings and books on architecture and classical antiquities. They returned by way of Geneva, which became the favoured city to spend winter during the tour. Here William became a central figure in the 'Common Room', a group of young English Grand Tourists who combined amateur theatricals with intrepid mountaineering on the Mer de Glace glacier near Chamonix, which he tried to describe: 'You must imagine your Lake put in Agitation by a strong Wind, and frozen all at once.'

While in Geneva, he became engaged to the daughter of a prominent local family, Elizabeth de Chapeaurouge, but thought better of it and only managed to escape from his impetuous proposal with considerable effort and expense. He may also have visited Vienna, because at some point on his travels he acquired an Austro-Hungarian hussar uniform in which he was painted in the swagger portrait now hanging in the Stair Hall. William returned home in 1742, but stayed away from Felbrigg until he inherited the estate on his father's death in 1749. Over the next twelve years he was to transform Felbrigg.

Left William Windham II in Hungarian hussar uniform , attributed to James Dagnia (c.1708/9–55). He based the composition on a painting now in the V&A by Thomas Worlidge of David Garrick as *Tancred* (Stair Hall)

A new interior

A passionate theatre-goer, William Windham II was a close friend and loyal ally of the great actor David Garrick, with whom he was painted by Francis Hayman relaxing in an English landscape setting. It was probably Hayman who introduced William to the architect James Paine. Paine's first task at Felbrigg was to design a new service wing, which combined improved accommodation for the servants with workshops for William's bookbinding, wood-turning and other practical activities. Paine added a bay-window at the north end of the west wing to provide a well-lit room, named the Cabinet, in which William could display the best of his Grand Tour views and Old Master purchases, together with superb Rococo mirrors, against crimson damask hangings.

William took a close interest in every detail of the project and couldn't hide his irritation when work ran late. He commissioned detailed diagrams showing where each picture should be hung, but still insisted on being present while this was being done. Where the 1680s staircase had been, he created a new dining-room as a tribute to the two previous generations of the family, whose portraits were hung here. The Dining Room was originally painted off-white but became a pale lilac in the 19th century, in contrast to the rich crimson and gold tones of the next-door Drawing Room. William retained the 1680s plasterwork ceiling of the Drawing Room. He took a similarly sympathetic attitude towards the Jacobean south wing, which many country-house owners

Above right Mrs Sarah Lukin (1710–92), who married William Windham II in 1750, painted by Rev. James Wills (Yellow Bedroom)

A hasty marriage

William had been living with a widow, Mrs Sarah Lukin, for several years when his father, who disapproved of the relationship, died in 1749. The main obstacle to their marriage had gone, and the matter became urgent when Mrs Lukin conceived a child in late 1749. To ensure that the baby was born legitimate, the couple were hastily married in February 1750. Three months later, a son, William Windham III, was safely delivered. There were to be no more siblings (Sarah was already 40). Once again, the future of the Windham line, and of Felbrigg, depended on a single child. William III was only eleven when his father died of TB in 1761.

The great explosion of 1755

William Windham II had a passion for fireworks, but the great explosion of 27 December 1755 probably brought Windham's interest in pyrotechnics to a premature end. It entirely destroyed his firework shop, whose roof was blown over the top of the granary and was later found blazing in the coalyard. Windows were smashed throughout the service yard, and everyone considerably shaken up. The room was never rebuilt, remaining single-storey to this day.

of the 1750s would have recast in a contemporary style. Instead, he contented himself with decorating the Great Hall in a plain neo-Tudor manner. On the floor immediately above, he commissioned Gothick-style bookcases for a new Library to house his rapidly expanding book collection.

Talented in life, tortured in love

William Windham III (1750–1810)

'In addition to his superiority in classical attainments, he was the best cricketer, the best leaper, swimmer, rower, skaiter, the best fencer, the best boxer, the best runner and the best horseman of his time.'

Edmond Malone on the young William Windham III

William Windham III was the first member of his family to be a national figure, but public success contrasted with personal unhappiness.

The best at everything

At Eton, where he was known as 'Fighting Windham', William showed immense promise. He became a close friend of the radical Charles James Fox – a friendship that survived their later political disagreements. His relationships with women were more complicated and ultimately frustrating. William became infatuated with Bridget Byng, the wife of the solitary travel writer John Byng, Viscount Torrington. His unrequited love, which was never consummated, caused him a great deal of unhappiness. Gradually, he transferred his affections to Bridget's sister Cecilia Forrest, who – to complicate matters further – had fallen in love with William's best friend George Cholmondeley, despite the fact that he had no intention of marrying her. This was all happening while William was trying to decide which career to follow. Eventually, after much heart-searching, he settled on politics.

Like Fox and his circle, he opposed the war with the American colonies. He first made his mark in 1778 with a speech in Norwich which was considered a masterpiece of oratory. The diarist Parson Woodforde, who was in the audience, noted: 'Most People admired the manner of Windham's speaking, so much Elegance, Fluency and Action in it.' Windham was briefly Chief Secretary for Ireland until illness cut short the posting. He was elected MP for Norwich in 1784 and four years later played a leading part in the

Left George James Cholmondeley (1752–1830) by Sir Joshua Reynolds, William Windham III's best friend and rival for the affections of Cecilia Forrest (Drawing Room)

Below William Windham III making his first important political speech, in Norwich in 1778. This sketch is by his aide Humphry Repton, later to become famous as a garden designer (Rose Bedroom)

Opposite The young William Windham III; pastel drawing by Hugh Douglas Hamilton (1740–1808), 1773 (Red Bedroom)

trial of the statesman Warren Hastings. He was an early enthusiast for the French Revolution, but, as an admirer of the conservative thinker Edmund Burke, gradually turned against it. When France declared war in 1793, he argued for a firm response. Between 1794 and 1801 he served in William Pitt's Cabinet as Secretary at War. In 1801 he resigned from office with the fall of the Pitt government, powerfully attacking the brief Peace of Amiens from the back benches. When Pitt returned to power in 1803, it was without Windham, who opposed the King's exclusion of Fox from government. For turning against Pitt, he was pilloried – somewhat unfairly – as 'Weathercock Windham', but he did not help his cause by objecting to a state funeral for Pitt after his sudden death in 1806.

Solitude and languor

Outwardly, William Windham III was firm in his views, but privately he was plagued with self-doubt, as he admitted in his diaries: 'This habit of indecision … wastes my time, consumes my strength, converts comfort into vexation and distress, deprives me of various pleasures, and involves me in innumerable difficulties.' It cannot have helped his self-confidence that his skin was disfigured by smallpox.

Windham's attitude to Felbrigg was similarly conflicted. He loved the place when he was away from it, which was most of the year. In his absence, Felbrigg was left in the capable hands of Nathaniel Kent, who was appointed agent for the estate in 1775, when he already had a reputation as a pioneering agricultural improver. Kent devoted much time and effort to planting new woodland and enclosing common land. But when Windham was staying in the house, he soon grew bored with the 'solitude and languor of Felbrigg', and longed to be back in London society.

After many years' hesitation, in 1798 William finally married Cecilia. By then, they were both in their late 40s, and so did not contemplate having children or making changes to their domestic arrangements. It is not surprising therefore that Windham did little to the house, compared with his father. In 1787–9 the architect Robert Furze Brettingham made various minor alterations. He filled in the west windows of the Great Hall and the Library, the latter to make room for even more bookshelves. Coloured glass was inserted in the remaining Library windows to prevent sunlight damaging the book spines. In 1809 a new Morning Room replaced the old kitchen at the east end of the south front, where it gets the best of the morning light.

For all his personal uncertainties, William Windham III was loyal to his friends and shared his father's passion for books. He kept a bedside vigil for Dr Johnson during his last days. It was his courageous efforts to rescue the library of his friend Frederick North from a house fire that caused the hip injury which led ultimately to his own death in 1810.

Left The monument to William Windham III by Joseph Nollekens (1737–1823) in Felbrigg church. It was installed in 1813 at a cost of £290

Left William Windham III in his later years; by John Jackson (1778–1831) after Thomas Lawrence. Windham's loyalty to his friends was demonstrated by his constant care during Dr Johnson's final illness in 1784. The Library still contains some of Johnson's books, given as keepsakes in recognition of Windham's equal devotion to learning (Drawing Room)

Luxury

Admiral William Lukin/Windham (1768–1833)

William Windham III bequeathed Felbrigg to his widow Cecilia for the remainder of her life, but as they had no children, on her death the estate passed to the eldest son of his half-brother, William Lukin (see family tree). Like Nelson, Lukin was the son of a Norfolk clergyman and he had a distinguished career in Nelson's navy, which was more meritocratic than most professions of that era. He first went to sea in 1781 as a thirteen-year-old midshipman. By 1795 he had been promoted to captain. In 1797 he helped to quell the Spithead mutiny by 'judicious management' of his crew. In 1806 he made his name as commander of the 75-gun ship of the line *Mars*, capturing four

Opposite Vice-Admiral
William Windham by
George Clint (1770–1854),
c.1825 (Stair Hall)

Below The service South
Corridor with Gothic
windows

Right Detail of the early
18th-century Boulle desk in
the Drawing Room, which is
typical of Admiral
Windham's taste

French troop ships in an action off Rochefort.
He retired from the navy as a Vice-Admiral in 1814
just as the Napoleonic Wars were coming to an
end.

It was to be another ten years before Cecilia
died and William could come into his inheritance.
In the interim, the Admiral travelled on the
Continent, where he bought marine paintings
that recalled his former life. Once he finally came
into Felbrigg (changing his surname to
Windham), he set to work modernising the
house, which had had little done to it since the
previous century. A local architect W.J. Donthorn
was commissioned to remodel Paine's service
quarters and build a neo-Tudor stable block.
Unfortunately, the work was done on the cheap,
which was to cause endless problems later on. He
also bought inlaid furniture in the lavish Regency
style and grand four-poster beds that brought a
touch of luxury to the house. The star piece is the
late 17th-century *bureau Mazarin* now in the
Drawing Room. All this work was done in the nine
years that the Admiral had left to him.

Improving the land

William Howe Windham (1802–54)

Like many of his ancestors, the Admiral's eldest son and heir, William Howe Windham, made the Grand Tour, in 1824–5. But unlike them, he did so with little enthusiasm, other than for opera. The diarist Charles Greville called him 'a rough unlettered squire', as his real passions were shooting and farming. In 1834 he and his shooting friends bagged more than 5,000 game birds. As a farmer, he modelled himself on the great north Norfolk improving landowner Coke of Holkham. He spent large sums on expanding the estate and putting up new farm buildings, lodges and cottages in the neo-Jacobean style, all carefully identified with date stones on the gable ends. He also remodelled the doorcases and the plasterwork ceiling of the Great Hall in the same emphatic style. The windows of this room were

filled with stained glass, both ancient originals from St Peter Mancroft in Norwich, and modern copies. Heraldic glass celebrated his marriage in 1835 to Lady Sophia Hervey of Ickworth (also NT). William Howe Windham achieved a great deal on the estate in a short time, dying in 1854 at the age of only 52 and leaving a young son, William Frederick, who was to bring Felbrigg to the brink of disaster.

Above William Howe Windham installed the neo-Jacobean doorcases in the Great Hall

Left William Howe Windham, English School (Morning Room)

Felbrigg in jeopardy

William Frederick Windham (1840–66)

William Frederick began behaving oddly at an early age. He was mercilessly teased at Eton, where his tutor recalled, 'He was looked upon by the boys as a buffoon, and he was generally called by them "Mad Windham".' Neglected by his parents, he was taken out of school and largely brought up in the servants' hall at Felbrigg, where he was allowed to serve at table in footman's livery, which he loved. While still at school, where he was nicknamed 'Gla', he showed a passion for trains. He would descend on Eton station with a whistle, and would play the role of guard, ticket collector, porter and even engine driver, causing predictable confusion.

When in London he haunted the Haymarket, then a notorious red-light district. At Ascot races in 1861 he first encountered an altogether higher-class courtesan. Agnes Willoughby cut a striking figure with a 26-inch waist and a scarlet riding habit. She and her pimp 'Bawdyhouse Bob' recognised Gla as an easy and lucrative catch, although the Felbrigg estates were already heavily mortgaged. Agnes and her cronies set about entrapping the besotted Gla into marriage. He splurged £14,000 on jewellery for his bride. If the estate was to be rescued from bankruptcy, his uncle and executor of his father's will, Lt-General Charles Ashe Windham, felt that he had no option but to launch a judicial inquiry into his nephew's mental health. The 34-day court case was the sensation of the 1861 season, with every unsavoury detail of Gla's unhappy life being dragged into the open. Despite this, Gla attracted a great deal of public sympathy, and he was eventually declared sane.

Above Agnes Willoughby, who entrapped William Frederick Windham into marriage (Stone Corridor)

Left William Frederick Windham as a boy, English School (Morning Room)

Unsurprisingly, the marriage did not last long, but it did in 1864 produce a son, Frederick, who was to inherit from his mother the Hanworth portion of the Felbrigg estates which she had been given by Gla. Gla was left with almost nothing, and even a measure of contentment as the driver of the express coach between Norwich and Cromer was short-lived – he was dismissed for wild driving. He died in poverty in 1866, aged only 26.

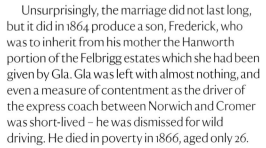

A self-made man

John Ketton (1808–72)

In 1863 the Felbrigg estate, the house and its entire contents were sold for £77,238 7s 1d to John Ketton, a Norwich merchant who had grown rich selling oil-cake and other cattle feedstuff.

It was then not only unusual for an estate and the entire contents of its house to come on the market, but it was also extremely rare for a tradesman to acquire such an estate. It caused quite a stir in the locality.

John Ketton's wife Rachel Anne Blake came from a Norfolk Quaker family. Like many Quakers, Rachel kept a diary, which recorded her family's modest and uneventful social life. Fortunately for us, the Kettons were content to live on the surface of the house, retaining Felbrigg's historic contents, making few changes and enduring the bitter Norfolk winters without complaint. John was more active outside, creating the American Garden north of the house as typical Victorian pleasure grounds with specimen transatlantic species. John Ketton's later years were soured by disputes with his eldest son John, which became so bad that he disinherited him, passing Felbrigg to his second son Robert William on his death in 1872.

Rachel Anne Ketton's diary

14th October 1863
Went to dine at Gurney Hoare's, 16 to dinner, all relations except ourselves – they played at making verses in the evening, and there was a great deal of laughing …

16th October
Mr Charles Buxton called for Anna and Minnie to join their riding party, they went on the sands and enjoyed it very much.

Above John Ketton, English School, c.1860, whose daughter Rachel Anna married into the Wyndham Cremer line in 1869 when she married Thomas Cremer in Felbrigg church (Morning Room)

Decline

Robert William Ketton (1854–1935)

Stopping the rot

Wyndham Cremer Ketton-Cremer
(1870–1933)

'A rather frustrated and decidedly eccentric old man' was how Robert Ketton was remembered by his great nephew. He was a radical in politics, which set him apart from his Tory neighbours and relations. He never married, but relied on his two youngest sisters, Marion and Gertrude, to keep house for him. Sadly, both died young in the 1890s, and he never really recovered from the loss. Robert became a recluse who retreated into a few rooms in the house. Decay set in everywhere, rain poured in through the roof of the house, and the farms and woodland were neglected. In 1918 he sold the Chinese porcelain, the Sèvres and the Meissen for paltry amounts. He also disposed of the best of the books and some of the fine Bladwell furniture from the Cabinet (see p. 42).

In 1924 Robert Ketton suddenly decided to move out of the house and hand over the entire estate to his nephew, Wyndham Cremer Cremer (Ketton was added after the handover). The decision to take on Felbrigg was by no means an easy one. Ketton-Cremer had just moved into Beeston Hall, of which his wife Emily was particularly fond. After 30 years of neglect, Felbrigg was in a desperate state – rat-infested and without electricity or bathrooms. Water was still raised from a well by a huge donkey-driven wheel. It was also a time of severe agricultural depression. But he decided to accept the challenge, and gradually Felbrigg was brought back from the brink of dereliction: land and an Old Master painting were sold to raise cash for repairs, roofs were mended, flowers bloomed in the garden once again, and trees were planted to fill the gaps in the woodland where timber had been felled during the First World War. Much-needed repairs were made to the church, where the monument to Thomas Windham (see p.9) was in danger of toppling over. However, all this work in late middle age put an inevitable strain on Ketton-Cremer's health, and he died in 1933, aged 63.

Above **Wyndham Cremer Ketton-Cremer**, who gave up the altogether more manageable house of Beeston Hall to save Felbrigg (Morning Room)

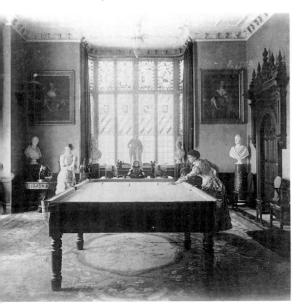

Left **Marion and Gertrude Ketton** playing billiards in the Great Hall in the 1870s

The last squire

Robert Wyndham Ketton-Cremer (1906–69)

R.W. Ketton-Cremer enjoyed a happy childhood at Beeston, but his time at Harrow and Oxford was blighted by bouts of rheumatic fever, which left him with a weakened right arm. However, this did not prevent him from enjoying shooting and the other pleasures of traditional rural life. He was also conscientious in fulfilling his responsibilities towards his staff and tenants. A traditionally minded but thoughtful Norfolk squire, he served as a JP and as High Sheriff of the county. More unusually for his class, he was also a scholar of 18th-century culture, replenishing the Felbrigg library, from which emerged a series of deeply researched books on Norfolk history. The finest of these is *Felbrigg: The Story of a House*, which is widely recognised as a classic of country-house literature. He was involved in the founding of the University of East Anglia, to which he bequeathed his books on Norfolk history.

Ketton-Cremer's first love was the woodland, which he revived, following his father's example. He also devoted time, money and imagination to repairing the house, the dove-house and the Orangery, which were equally dilapidated. The house came through the Second World War unscathed because of its very dereliction, which prevented it from being easily converted to military use. Electricity was finally installed in the house in 1954; it is typical of the man that his priority was to ensure that his tenants received electricity first. Ketton-Cremer never married, but assumed that his beloved younger brother Richard, known as Dick, would ultimately inherit and carry on the line. So it came as a devastating blow when Dick was killed during the German invasion of Crete in 1941. Even 20 years on, 'to read his letters is like the reopening of a wound'.

In *Felbrigg*, Ketton-Cremer concludes, 'I end the story here' – in May 1961. But this, of course, is not the end of the story. After the death of his brother, he found another solution to the future of Felbrigg in the National Trust, in whose work he had been involved since the late 1940s. On his death in 1969 he bequeathed Felbrigg complete with the garden, the estate and its historic collections to the National Trust, and all in better order than they had been for a century.

In the following decades, the Trust has carried out much careful conservation work at Felbrigg, guided by the last squire's example. Mature woodland has been replenished, heathland created and fragile fabrics repaired. The planting in the Walled Garden has been refreshed, and the ceiling of the Library has been restored to its original form.

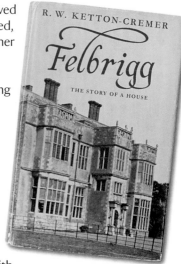

Above *Felbrigg: The Story of a House* was published by Rupert Hart-Davis in 1962 and has become a classic among books about the country house

'…his portly figure made even more shapeless by an old macintosh, his grey hair straggling beneath a green pork-pie hat, his slightly gouty step supported by a walking-stick.'

Brinsley Ford on the last squire of Felbrigg

Above Robert Wyndham
Ketton-Cremer by the front
door of Felbrigg

Left Robert Wyndham
Ketton-Cremer; painted by
Allan Gwynne-Jones
(1892–1982) in the Dining
Room. The painting is in the
Great Hall

The House

Limestone, brick, render, flint, iron: these are just some of the materials from which Felbrigg was built, and all have been mellowed by the Norfolk weather.

The South Front

This is the earliest part of the present house, which was begun in 1620 on the site of the Tudor predecessor, fragments of which can still be seen in the basement. The carcass is red brick with mullions and doorcases in limestone from Ketton in Rutland. It has similarities with Blickling Hall, which was being built at the same time, employing many of the same craftsmen and almost certainly the same architect – Robert Lyminge. The cut-out Latin lettering high on the rooftop balustrade boldly proclaims the glory of God in the highest. The idea seems to have been French in origin, and if so, was just one of many continental influences on Felbrigg. Render was applied to the brickwork when built and reapplied in 1825 by W.J. Donthorn, but has been falling off ever since.

The West Wing

This extends at right-angles to the south front, and was designed in a very different, Restoration

Below The south front. The Jacobean desire for symmetry is reflected in the identical chimneystacks

style by the gentleman-architect William Samwell for William Windham I. Samwell presented his first plans in 1674, but did not live to see the wing completed, probably in the mid-1680s. It was constructed of very finely laid red brick; the tall sash-windows seem to have been an afterthought. The dormer and bay windows, together with the Westmorland slate roof, were part of James Paine's remodelling in the 1750s for William Windham II.

The East Wing

The service wing, which extends eastwards from the south front, was designed by Paine in a contrasting Palladian style in 1751 (see pp. 22–3). Like many such staff quarters, it features a clock-tower to encourage good time-keeping. What was originally an open arcade below was enclosed by Donthorn in 1825 to form a more comfortable service corridor.

The Stable Block

At the same time Donthorn also designed new stables beyond Paine's service wing in yet another style – castellated neo-Tudor. The red brick was originally rendered, but this has long since fallen off; the Admiral's attempt at economy has resulted in much subsequent expense. Well into the era of the motor car, the stables housed the family's horses and carriages, but have now largely been given over to the tea-room and shop.

Above The Stable Block. The central section housed the carriages, while horses were stabled in the wings. The screen is comparable with a much finer one designed by William Wilkins for King's College, Cambridge

Inside Felbrigg: the Collections

On their travels, generations of Windhams acquired beautiful paintings and furniture to display in Felbrigg's handsome rooms.

Above Detail of the Drawing Room carpet: an English 'Savonnerie' pattern of c.1851

Left The picture-hang of William Windham II's Grand Tour paintings in the Cabinet has changed little since his time

Far left Regency sofa in the Drawing Room

Left Late 17th-century *bureau Mazarin*, decorated with elaborate Boulle-work marquetry

Above The marble head of the radical politician Charles James Fox is one of the series of late 18th-century 'political' busts collected by William Howe Windham. A notorious gambler and drinker, Fox died at Chiswick House, London

Left *The Battle of the Texel (1673): the Engagement of the Two Fleets* by Willem van de Velde the Elder (1611–93), bought by William Windham II

The Family Rooms

The Screens Passage

This entrance corridor is a throwback to large medieval houses. It connects the Great Hall of the Jacobean house (on the left) with what would originally have been the pantry, buttery and servery of the servants' quarters (on the right).

The mid-18th-century hall-chairs are decorated with the Windham coat of arms and were originally part of the furnishings of the Great Hall. They were not upholstered so as to be hard-wearing and easy to keep clean.

The Morning Room

This was created from the kitchen and service rooms of the Jacobean house. It became a parlour in 1809, when the panelling was installed. The room faces south and east and so gets the best of the morning sun. The present decoration probably dates from the mid-19th century.

Pictures

These are mostly early to mid-19th-century Windham portraits. Over the fireplace hangs a group portrait of Captain (later Vice-Admiral) William Lukin setting out for a day's shooting from Felbrigg Parsonage with his brothers and Cawston the gamekeeper (kneeling). Lukin lived here while on shore leave and while waiting (somewhat impatiently) to inherit Felbrigg, which he finally did in 1824, when he took the Windham name. Felbrigg church can be seen in the distance.

Above the Lukin group is an individual portrait of Admiral Lukin in naval uniform. His swashbuckling career reads like a Hornblower novel (see p.22). To the left is a portrait of the Admiral's son and heir, William Howe Windham, who energetically modernised the Felbrigg estate in the 1840s. Over the door to the Lobby hangs a portrait of William Frederick 'Mad' Windham as a boy. His eccentric behaviour provoked a scandalous court case and his eventual bankruptcy (see p.25).

Ceramics

In the glazed bureau-bookcase is a Meissen porcelain service, the plates and dishes painted with birds and flowers, c.1755–60.

Clock

By the door from the Screens Passage is a late 19th-century eight-day clock in solid walnut case, reputedly made from timber grown on the estate.

Opposite Captain William Lukin (in the centre) and his brothers set out from Felbrigg Parsonage for a day's shooting, by William Redmore Bigg, 1803

Right The Morning Room

Below Detail of the white marble chimneypiece, c.1850, in the Morning Room

'I always have a few ginger plants, as I like to have their musky scent wafting through the house.'

R.W. Ketton-Cremer

The Great Hall

By 1833 the Great Hall of the Jacobean house was being used as a billiards room. It took its present form in 1842, when William Howe Windham remodelled the room in heavy neo-Jacobean style with ornate doorcases and a plasterwork ceiling decorated with wooden pendants. The overmantel combines an oval heraldic panel of the 1620s with a Victorian cartouche of curling strapwork.

To the left of the fireplace is a portrait of Sir William Paston, who filled his Norfolk home, Oxnead Hall, with collections of pictures and curiosities. In the 1630s Paston travelled to Egypt, where he encountered the crocodile shown in the background.

Stained glass

William Howe Windham also installed the stained glass, which is a complicated mixture of original medieval panels removed from St Peter Mancroft, Norwich, and early Victorian copies. There are also fragments of religious and heraldic glass made on the Continent.

Pictures

The portraits are mainly of 17th-century Windhams, their friends, relations and neighbours. To the right of the fireplace hangs a

'Although our visit took place in May [1953] it was still far too cold to inhabit the grand suite of rooms in the west wing, so we lived and had all our meals in the Great Hall. This was heated fairly effectively by a large and ugly anthracite stove round which we sat on the few chairs that were not piled high with books.'

Brinsley Ford

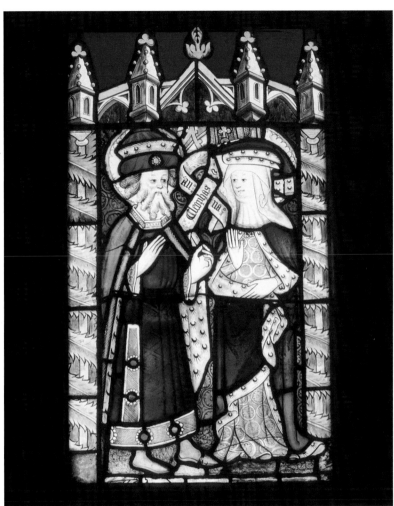

probable portrait of William Windham I painted in the 1680s at the end of his life by Sir Godfrey Kneller. To the left of the doorway as you come in is R.W. Ketton-Cremer, the last squire of Felbrigg, who devoted his life to saving the house, garden and estate and writing about their history. He was painted by Allan Gwynne-Jones in the Dining Room next door (see p. 29), where the afternoon light is particularly good, but it was left unfinished at the sitter's death – it is said, because the artist did not want to end his agreeable visits to Felbrigg.

Sculpture

The marble busts include those great political adversaries of the late 18th century, William Pitt the younger (with pointed nose and receding chin) and Charles James Fox (fat and swarthy). William Windham III (whose bust is also here) served in Pitt's Cabinet as Secretary at War, but was reluctant to abandon his friendship with Fox, giving rise to his nickname, 'Weathercock Windham'. Military adversaries are represented by the busts of the Duke of Wellington and Napoleon.

From the Great Hall you enter the west wing, which was built by William Windham I in the 1680s and transformed by his grandson William Windham II into the present suite of handsome reception rooms in the 1750s.

The Dining Room

In 1752 William Windham II commissioned his architect James Paine to replace the main staircase of the 1680s wing with a dining room. Originally off-white, the walls were repainted in pale lilac in the 19th century. The off-white of the plaster mouldings, doors and window surrounds dates from 1824.

Rachel Ketton noted in her diary for 24 August 1863: 'Although the dinner passed off pretty well, the haunch was entirely spoiled by being over cooked.'

Plasterwork

The plaster ceiling is the work of the master plasterer Joseph Rose the Elder and his assistant George Green. It was put up in 1752, although the style of framing is of the 1680s. Appropriately for an eating room, the subjects are the natural world: the central panel is of an eagle, above the doors are symbols of the chase and the corners feature heads symbolising the four seasons – spring (flowers), summer (ears of corn), autumn (grapes), winter (bearded head).

The wall plasterwork frames oval mirrors and family portraits and includes lead chains that reference the Felbriggs' arms fetterlock emblem which the Windhams adopted.

The chimneypiece is made of cheaper hard stucco, not marble, as first appears. Again appropriately for a dining room, it is decorated with grapes and vine leaves.

Pictures

William Windham II conceived the room as a tribute to his parents and grandparents, and their portraits have not been moved since they were first hung here in the 1750s, despite the bank

foreclosure and the sale of house and contents in 1863. They include, over the mantelpiece, Sir Joseph Ashe, a wealthy merchant whose daughter Katherine married William Windham I in 1669. Portraits of Katherine and William flank the door to the Drawing Room beyond. Their son and heir Ashe hangs to the right of the door from the Great Hall. The portrait to the left of the door may be of Elizabeth Dobyns, who married Ashe in 1709; she soon fell out with him and they eventually separated. The oval portrait over the door to the Great Hall is of Ashe's younger brother Colonel William Windham, who lost a leg at the battle of Blenheim in 1704 during the War of Spanish Succession. He endured the amputation with extraordinary stoicism.

Above The Dining Room, looking through to the Drawing Room

Right Detail of the central panel of the ceiling

Far right Wall panel with portrait of Ashe Windham by Sir Godfrey Kneller

'The food was not as imaginative as the decoration. But it was English food at its best. And who could want anything better than lobsters from Sheringham, lamb cutlets with broad beans or peas or asparagus freshly picked from the garden, followed by gooseberry or red-currant pie with cream from the farm. The cellar was well-stocked with fine clarets and port, and given Wyndham's abstemious habits there was never any chance of it running dry.'

Brinsley Ford

The Drawing Room

This was originally the oak-panelled main reception and dining room, known as the Great Parlour until the 19th century. It was remodelled in 1751 by Paine, who supplied the richly carved doorcases and dadoes, but retained the 1680s ceiling (see box). William Windham II used the room to display the best and largest of his Grand Tour purchases. The marble fireplace of 1751 was originally tried in the Cabinet next door. Flanking it are gilt Rococo candle brackets in the form of mermen, in keeping with the maritime flavour of the room. Admiral Windham put up the crimson damask wall-hangings in about 1830 and had the sofa, chairs and fire-screens upholstered to match. The grandest piece of furniture in the room is the late 17th-century French *bureau Mazarin* decorated with elaborate Boulle-work marquetry. The early 19th-century New Hall teapot was a present to the last squire's mother from Queen Mary, who was a passionate country-house visitor.

A plasterwork feast

The superb plasterwork ceiling survives from William Windham I's original room: it is dated in Roman numerals 1687. It was probably made by Edward Goudge, who was doing work of similar quality at Belton in Lincolnshire at the same time (also NT). The subject-matter reflects the room's original use as a dining room. Local game birds of the kind William Windham I would have shot on the estate fill the corner compartments, including pheasants, partridges, mallard, woodcock and plovers. There are also beautifully modelled fruit, flowers and seashells.

Above left The Drawing Room; the carpet is an 'English Savonnerie' design of *c.*1851

Above *The Thames by the Tower of London* by Samuel Scott, who became known as 'the English Canaletto' for his pictures of the river. Horace Walpole had a large collection of his paintings and said they 'will charm in any age'. The prominent vessel in the foreground is a Danish timber vessel known as a 'cat bark'

Pictures

Above the chimneypiece hangs John Jackson's copy of Sir Thomas Lawrence's unfinished 1802–3 portrait of William Windham III, who is depicted as the statesman he had become. He was the only member of the family to be a national political figure, and as a result spent little time at Felbrigg. Despite a successful political career, he considered himself to be a perpetual outsider – 'a scholar among politicians and a politician among scholars'.

To the left of the fireplace in the middle is Reynolds's portrait of Windham's closest friend, George Cholmondeley, with whom Cecilia Forrest, Windham's future wife, was in love.

The end walls are filled by William Windham II's large marine and topographical views. Flanking the door to the Dining Room are two paintings of the Battle of the Texel: to the left of

the door is *The bombardment of the Royal Prince (1673)* by Willem van de Velde the Elder and Younger; and to the right of the door *The engagement of the two fleets (1673)* by Willem van de Velde the Elder. The battle was the last major engagement of the three Anglo-Dutch wars. Ketton-Cremer was obliged to sell the left-hand picture in 1934 to pay death duties and for repairs. It has kindly been loaned back by the National Maritime Museum.

On the opposite wall are Samuel Scott's two Thames-side views. *Old London Bridge* shows the famous river crossing when it still had houses on it; these were pulled down in 1757, four years after this picture was painted. The other view, *The Thames by the Tower of London*, was painted between 1746 and 1753, when William Windham II commissioned matching frames for the two pictures.

The Cabinet

Originally, this was the 'Drawing Room', to which the family and their guests would 'withdraw' after dining in the Great Parlour next door. The bay window was added in 1751, when William Windham II transformed the room as the setting for his smaller Grand Tour pictures and the climax to the suite of grand reception rooms that ran along the west front.

Ceiling

The outer section is the original and was probably made by Edward Goudge about 1687. The plan is similar to Goudge's later ceiling at Belton. The central compartment and that over the bay window were designed by James Paine and put up in 1750–1.

Decoration

The Cabinet provided the red, white and gold theme later adopted for the Drawing Room. The crimson worsted damask wall-hangings survive from 1751 in remarkably good condition.

Furnishings

The magnificent gilt overmantel mirror and picture frame were made by John Bladwell in 1752. The ormolu (gilt brass) candle branches and gilt plaster wall-brackets match those in the Drawing Room.

Pictures

This room is a very rare surviving example of an 18th-century Grand Tour collection still displayed as originally intended. The six large oil paintings and 26 small gouaches of Rome and its surroundings were commissioned from Giovanni Battista Busiri by William Windham II while he was in Rome in 1739. Plans in the family archives reveal the care he took in framing and hanging these views of the Eternal City.

Far left Rococo pier-table, made by a London cabinetmaker, perhaps James Whittle or Thomas Chippendale

Left The Cabinet

Below *The Ponte Nomentano* by Giovanni Battista Busiri (1698–1757). Built on the site of a Roman bridge, the tower structure dates from the 15th century and protects the northern approach to the city by the Via Nomentana where it crosses the River Aniene

The Grand Tour

During the 18th century, rich young Englishmen often finished their education by touring the Continent. They usually took in the historic cities of Italy, including Rome, where they could absorb the greatest works of classical and Renaissance art at first hand. For some, it was merely an excuse for a drunken binge, but others, like William Windham II, took the journey more seriously, buying books, refining their critical faculties and acquiring paintings, sculpture and furniture to decorate their homes back in Britain.

The Stone Corridor

This and the West Corridor immediately above were added in 1751 by William Windham II to allow more discreet access to the rooms in the west wing. The decoration is modern. The portrait of a lady is Agnes Willoughby, 'Mad' Windham's wife (see p.25).

Ceramics

The 18th-century 'Bordaloues' (chamberpots designed specifically for women) in the display cabinet are a reminder of the days before modern plumbing and *en suite* bathrooms.

The Stair Hall

In 1752 Paine replaced the original 1680s staircase with the present arrangement and a handsome iron balustrade. It resembles the Dining Room next door in featuring bronzed plaster busts of ancient Greek and Roman worthies in oval niches. The wall colour, devised by Admiral Lukin in 1824, is also similar.

At the bottom of the stairs is a marble sculpture known as the *Il Spinario* (*Boy pulling a Thorn out of his Foot*). It is one of the most famous (and most copied) statues to have come down to us from antiquity. According to legend, it commemorates a shepherd boy called Martius, who was ordered to bring a message to the Roman Senate and only stopped to remove a thorn from his foot when he had completed the task.

Right The Stair Hall with two of the bronzed plaster busts of real or imagined likenesses of Ancient Greeks and Romans by John Cheere (1709–87)

Puzzling portraits: The 'gentleman glassblower' and the hussar

Two large full-length portraits hang on the upper landing. 'Count' James Dagnia (*c*.1708/9–55) came from a family of Italian glassmakers who settled in County Durham. He later moved to Rome, where he acquired a title and was much patronised by British Grand Tourists such as William Windham II. Dagnia seems to have sat for one of these portraits and painted the other – of Windham in the uniform of an Austro-Hungarian hussar. Was Windham simply dressing up, or did he serve in a Viennese cavalry regiment? We do not know.

Above 'Count' James Dagnia painted by John Shackleton

Above *Il Spinario*, a 19th-century copy of the Antique bronze which has been in the Palazzo dei Conservatori on the Capitol in Rome since the 15th century

The Library

William Windham II turned this room into the Library in 1752–5 to house his rapidly growing collection. James Paine designed the oak bookcases in the Gothick style, which Windham thought was appropriate to a Jacobean house. The Library occupies the west end of the original house's first floor. When William Windham III ran out of space for his books, he blocked up the west-bay window and filled it with shelves.

Restoring the ceiling

In 1924, after years of neglect, the Ketton-Cremers replaced Paine's neo-Jacobean plasterwork ceiling with a plain, flat one. When fragments of the original ceiling were discovered above the blocked-up west-bay window in 1999, it was decided to re-create Paine's scheme, drawing on all the physical and documentary evidence. The work was undertaken by Stevensons of Norwich, using traditional materials and techniques. The room is whole once more.

Books

Despite sales in 1919, Felbrigg still possesses one of the most interesting libraries in the care of the National Trust, as several members of the family were obsessive book collectors. William Windham I owned a copy of the first edition of John Evelyn's *Sylva* (1664), which guided his replanting of the Felbrigg woods. His wife Katherine collected plays by Dryden and his contemporaries. In 'A note of my Books' she listed her acquisitions, more than half of which were religious.

William Windham II's purchases, which comprise the heart of the library, reflect his wide interests, his travels and his friendships. He returned from his Grand Tour of 1738–42 laden with handsome folio volumes on architecture and antiquities. He was also one of the original subscribers to Stuart and Revett's *Antiquities of Athens* (1762), a key source book for the Neo-

classical style. He was given the manuscript of his friend David Garrick's play *Ragandjaw* (1746), which was dedicated to him. He also took a practical interest in the appearance of his books, owning a copy of Gauffecourt's treatise on bookbinding and a set of bookbinding tools.

As one might expect from a politician, William Windham III bought books on philosophy, politics and economics. He was a devoted friend of the great lexicographer Samuel Johnson, who

Below The Library looking towards the Book Room (beyond the white door). The much-worn and faded carpet of the 1840s has recently been replaced by a replica expertly woven by the Living Looms Project to match the rich colours of the original

Right The celestial and terrestrial globes made by J. & W. Cary of 181 The Strand in 1799 and 1814 respectively

Below right Access to the water closet in the Library is disguised by a jib door – a door that matches the panelling

'… in a room adjoining it [the Library] Mr Windham always sat when engaged in business or study … During this time he slept in a small tent bed put up in a niche in a room next to His sitting room, for the convenience of it being near the Library.'

The diarist Joseph Farington (1747–1821)

bequeathed Windham his own copies of Homer and the New Testament. Windham also lent books on natural history from his library to Humphry Repton, who noted: 'his library has introduced me to Buffon, De Reaumur [both still in the library] &c; and they have brought me acquainted to all the insects in my neighbourhood.' The Victorian owners of Felbrigg were not bookish, and Robert Ketton was obliged to sell books to raise cash to repair the house. It was left to the last squire to fill the worst of the gaps and to assemble the impressive working library of a scholar and historian, part of which he bequeathed to the University of East Anglia.

The miniature bookcase contains a small collection of books thought suitable for the staff. Published by the Religious Tract Society, they have such uplifting titles as *The Faithful Servant*.

Globes

The pair of celestial and terrestrial globes dates from 1799 and 1814 respectively. The tripod stands incorporate compasses.

The Book Room

In the 1780s William Windham III converted this room, which you enter through a jib-door concealed in a bookcase, into a private study. It had been Sarah Windham's bedroom in the 1750s. It is now used to display some of the house's many treasures.

The Grey Dressing Room

We now re-enter the 1680s wing. An open cupboard door shows the 1680s plasterwork, and the panelling was installed in 1753 by William Windham II, who used it as a dressing room. The Rococo overmantel mirror was probably made by John Bladwell c.1750. The 'slipper' bath is Victorian.

The Yellow Bedroom

Like the Grey Dressing Room, this was created from the old stair hall in 1752–3 by William Windham II.

Pictures

The pastel portrait of William Windham II was painted by the Swiss artist Barthélémy du Pan, probably in Geneva, where he spent the winter of 1740–1 while on his Grand Tour. Today, we usually try to protect fabrics from the fading effects of sunlight, but Jan van Kessel's painting, *A bleaching-ground outside Haarlem*, shows laundry that has deliberately been left to dry and bleach in the sun.

Below *A bleaching-ground outside Haarlem* by Jan van Kessel. The picture was acquired by William Windham II in the Low Countries on his way back from Switzerland in 1742

> 'The brass can filled with hot water, which Ward [the butler] produced in the morning and again in the evening when one went up to dress for dinner, was always a welcome sight.'
>
> Brinsley Ford

Fabric refreshed

The rose chintz and lining fabric of the bed-hangings, curtains, pelmets and loose covers were introduced about 1840 by the Admiral, along with the mahogany bed and much of the other furniture. By 2004 the fabric had faded beyond repair, and so the Trust decided to reprint it using traditional methods and modern technology, following the colour of a small area of unfaded material at the bottom of a curtain.

Above The Rose Bedroom. The half-tester bed dates from *c*.1840

The Rose Bedroom

The plaster cove and border is probably Edward Goudge's work of *c*.1687, rearranged by George Green *c*.1752–3.

Pictures

Left of the bed hangs a pencil sketch of *William Windham III making his maiden speech in Norwich in 1778*. It was drawn by Humphry Repton, the influential garden designer who began his career as Windham's political secretary. Windham made his reputation in politics speaking against the war with the American colonies.

Furniture

The two white and gilt Bladwell mirrors, *c*.1752, incorporate late 17th-century bevelled mirror glass, which was still so expensive that it was worth reusing.

The serpentine-back sofa dates from *c*.1750.

The Red Bedroom

The flock and gilt striped wallpaper was hung about 1860, and has faded badly: the buff-coloured stripes were originally pink.

Furniture

The oval overmantel mirror was probably designed by Paine c.1752. In September 1751 William Windham II wrote, 'I find it is a high fashion for oval glasses to be placed over chimneys and carved work above them.'

The Chinese Bedroom

This room is immediately above the Cabinet at the north end of the west wing. William Windham II added the bay window in 1751, but retained the original ceiling.

Decoration

The Chinese wallpaper, which gives the room its name, was probably supplied by Paine in 1751 and hung by John Scruton, a London specialist who charged 3s 6d a day and 6d per mile travelling expenses, 'which I think a cursed deal', William Windham II complained. The outlines were printed and then coloured by hand. Some of the birds were cut from separate sheets and then pasted on.

On the wall-brackets is displayed a pair of 'nodding head' Chinese mandarin figures made for the western market c.1820.

The West Corridor

This was added in 1751–2 to allow better access to the west-wing bedrooms.

Furnishings

The walnut-veneer writing-desk was possibly that bought new by Katherine Windham in 1690/1. The mahogany chest, c.1800, probably belonged to the Admiral.

Right **The Chinese Bedroom**

Above **The Chinese wallpaper in the Chinese Bedroom**

Above **The Red Bedroom. The dado panelling and cornice date from** *c.*1705

The Bathroom

The Ketton-Cremers probably turned this into a bathroom in the 1920s. The pattern of the old lino suggests that it may have previously been a nursery.

Furniture

The lacquer screen dates from about 1700, the red lacquer bureau from about 1730.

The Back Stairs

The stairs were built in 1751, reusing balusters salvaged from the demolished Great Stair of the 1680s.

The Bird Corridor

This corridor was added in 1831 by Admiral Windham to make sure that food from the Kitchen arrived hot in the Dining Room. Prior to this the windows for both the Butler's Pantry and the China Room would have therefore been external. The corridor takes its name from the cases of stuffed birds, which were collected by Thomas Wyndham Cremer (1834–94), the last squire's grandfather, who was a keen ornithologist.

The headless lady

This Pentelic marble draped female figure comes from an important Athenian grave monument, c.350–320 BC. It was first noted at Felbrigg in the Walled Garden in 1847, when it was said to have been 'lately dug up on the plains of Troy'. It is similar in style to the Parthenon frieze in Athens and may have arrived at Felbrigg via Philip Hunt, chaplain to the Earl of Elgin. Hunt encouraged Elgin to remove the frieze sculptures from the Parthenon, and in his later years he became vicar of nearby Aylsham.

Above The Bathroom lino

Left The headless lady

Opposite The Bird Corridor showing the once external windows of the Butler's Pantry on the right. The bird displays were created in the second half of the 19th century by Norwich's principal taxidermist, Thomas Gunn of St Giles Street, and by Pratt & Sons of Brighton

The Working Rooms

The Butler's Pantry
This room dates from *c*.1750 and is fitted out with cupboards for glassware.

The China Room
This was fitted out *c*.1750 with oak cupboards and shelves and Delft tiles around the fireplace on the west wall. The blue-and-white plates, bowls and dishes displayed here are 18th-century.

You are now entering the servants' quarters, which have changed little since early Victorian times, when a house like Felbrigg had to be self-sufficient in so many ways. A separate room was provided for every domestic task: Game Larder, Bake House, Pump House, Brew House, Dairy, Wash House, Larder, Scullery – and that is just to list the rooms that you do *not* see!

The Kitchen
The Kitchen has been on this spot since the early 18th century. There are two long oak tables, one of which is 18th-century, the other Victorian. The last squire installed the Aga. The pewter and highly polished copper *batterie de cuisine* are typical of historic country-house kitchens.

'The house was run on old-fashioned lines by a staff of three. This consisted of [Gordon] Ward, the butler, who had already been at Felbrigg for thirty years, a maid and a cook.'

Brinsley Ford, 1950s

Left **The Kitchen**

Above **Copper pots and pans**

To Make an Orenge puding

Take a good Orenge, pare it very thin & split it, take out ye seeds & skin, take 2 halfes of Candied orenge peel, beat all very well in a Stone Morter y^n put to it 3 qu of a pound of fine loafe suger, continue beating, y^n add 3 quarters of a po of Buter 6 eggs with 4 of y^e Whites, when all these are well beaten together, put it in a dish with puffe past, under & over it, bake it in a gentle oven.

From Katherine Windham's
A Booke of Cookery & Houskeeping, 1707

The South Corridor

The fire at Clandon Park in Surrey in November 2015 is a sad reminder of this ever-present danger, especially in country-house kitchens. One rudimentary precaution at Felbrigg was the set of leather and metal fire buckets. They bear Rachel Anne Ketton's initials (which must have been applied in 1872–5 during her widowhood), but the leather ones date from the 18th century, the metal ones from the 19th. They may have been introduced following the great fireworks explosion in 1755 (see p.17). The late 18th-century fire-engine (essentially, a water pump on wheels) was designed to be operated by 2–4 men.

A servant's life at Felbrigg in the 1930s

In the 1930s there were three women employed in the Kitchen: the cook, kitchen maid and scullery maid. The butler ran the whole establishment, which also included two house maids, a chauffeur, an odd-job man and 3 or 4 gardeners. For the staff, it was a long day which began at 6am, and didn't finish till midnight, if there were guests. It was hard physical work: buckets of coal and pails of hot water had to be carried by hand up to the bedrooms. On special occasions, the maids wore coffee-coloured aprons, cap, cuffs and a wine-coloured dress.

Derived from an oral reminiscence of Mrs Molly Kirby, housemaid in the 1930s

Opposite The leather and metal fire buckets bearing Rachel Anne Ketton's initials

Right The late 18th-century fire-engine in the South Corridor

The Servants' Hall

The Servants' Hall and the Steward's Room still have much of the furniture made for them in the 1750s.

The Steward's Room

The estate was administered from this room by the steward (land agent) until 1970, when John Mottram took up the post for the National Trust.

The Tenants' Waiting Room

The Felbrigg estate's tenant farmers would assemble here to pay their rent on the four quarterdays: Lady Day (25 March), Midsummer (24 June), Michaelmas (29 September) and Christmas Day (25 December).

The Turnery

William Windham II enjoyed working with his hands and used this room for the popular 18th-century pastime of wood- and ivory-turning. He also stored his arsenal of sporting weapons here, which numbered 42 guns in the upper shop alone. The room above contained his book-binding and gilding tools.

The Turnery fireplace is decorated with stone tablets taken from buildings put up on the Felbrigg estate by William Howe Windham.

The Garden

The Walled Garden is both decorative and productive, growing flowers to adorn the house and fruit and vegetables on the community allotments.

The Rose Garden

This was laid out in 1971 in front of the east wing in memory of the last squire. However, over the years, the roses died. The profile of the gable which looks on to the Rose Garden was used as the inspiration for the shape of the borders.

The West Garden

The Orangery

This plain red-brick building was probably designed by Ashe Windham and completed by 1707. In the 18th century the sash-windows would have slid up from floor level, perhaps enabling orange trees in pots to be wheeled out onto the lawn in front for the summer. In the 19th century it was transformed into a Victorian conservatory with a glazed roof, which later suffered from neglect. The missing cedar shingle roof was replaced by the last squire in 1958. Today, the Orangery houses a fine collection of camellias, some of considerable size and age.

The American Garden

This typical Victorian pleasure ground lies west and north of the house and the Orangery. It was probably created in the 1860s for Felbrigg's new owner, John Ketton. It is planted with specimen trees, many from the Americas, such as the American buckeye, the Wellingtonia and the western red cedars.

The Walled Garden

Felbrigg possesses one of the finest walled gardens in East Anglia, situated to the north-east of the house. The earliest surviving feature is the

octagonal dove-house of 1753, which was an important source of fresh meat before the era of mechanical refrigeration. (The ice house in the Great Wood preserved lake ice for the kitchen.) The interior of the dove-house contains 2,000 nesting boxes. It was rescued from almost total dereliction by the last squire in 1937.

The east and west walls were rebuilt by the Admiral in 1825, using some of the bricks from the original 18th-century walls. His son William Howe Windham added the central circular pond and the cross-wall with its pine-cone finials. He also reused 17th-century stonework from the house to create the doorway in the south wall.

Above The double border in the Walled Garden

Right The dove-house and central pond in the Walled Garden. A Latin inscription on the dove-house records its restoration by the last squire

Far right Community allotments within the Walled Garden

'This region is from the superior fertility of the soil with propriety called the Garden of Norfolk.'

Humphry Repton, 1787

The borders to the east and west of the dove-house are largely given over to a wide variety of dyeing, medicinal and culinary herbs. Some of the clipped box hedges in the Walled Garden became infected with box blight and were replaced with lavender in 2013. The other borders are mixed herbaceous, with espaliered fruit trees such as plums, apples, figs and nectarines trained against the walls. More surprisingly, the olive trees here tolerate the worst of the north Norfolk winters. Bringing a delightful touch of informality are the bantams that scratch about the Walled Garden.

As part of the government initiative to encourage people to grow their own food, some community allotments have been created here.

The Greenhouses
Only two of the formerly extensive range of glasshouses survived the neglect of the Walled Garden in the early 20th century. Both houses were repaired in 2004.

The Park

The open parkland to the south of the house dates back to the Middle Ages, when it was maintained as a deer-park for hunting. Today, there are four types of deer to be seen at Felbrigg: roe, red, muntjac and Chinese water.

In contrast to the park is the Great Wood to the north, which was developed by William Windham I in the 1670s–80s as a shelterbelt against the prevailing northerly gales. Following the lead of John Evelyn's influential handbook on trees, *Sylva*, Windham chose commercial varieties of conifer as well as more ornamental deciduous species. He also repaired and extended the park wall. The Great Wood was progressively enlarged during the course of the next two centuries.

At the heart of the Great Wood is the ice house, which was probably built in the 18th century, reusing 17th-century bricks from a collapsed section of the old park wall. It looks like a ruin, but in fact was built in this form.

Between 1770 and 1788 William Windham III's pioneering steward Nathaniel Kent planted at least thirteen new woods. The landscape designer Humphry Repton began his career as Windham's political secretary and he may have had some say in the development of the park. Little documentary evidence survives of his involvement, but it seems likely, because the park, with its clumps and belts of trees, is characteristic of Repton's style.

Like the rest of the estate, the woodland suffered neglect in the late 19th and early 20th centuries, with little being done to replace the over-mature timber. Revival came with the Ketton-Cremers in the mid-1920s, followed by the last squire, who was passionate about his woodland. Major features were the avenues he cut through the Great Wood in the shape of a 'Victory V' to commemorate the death of his beloved brother. The arms of the V frame a distant view of the spire of Norwich Cathedral. The National Trust has followed in the last squire's footsteps in restoring lost features and creating new ones. It has returned much of the parkland from arable to traditional pasture.

Above Invisible from the house, Felbrigg lake was created in the mid-18th century by damming the Scarrow Beck. Tench, rudd, eel and pike live in the four-acre lake. Among the birds attracted to the water are Egyptian goose, kingfisher, little grebe, moorhen and coot

Opposite Autumnal scene in the Great Wood, once part of the old deer-park

St Margaret's Church

Today the Felbrigg parish church (not NT) stands in isolation in the south-east corner of the park. It may have been surrounded by Felbrigg village, which was swept away in the 17th century, perhaps to exterminate an outbreak of plague. The early 15th-century west tower bears the lion and fetterlock emblems of Sir Simon Felbrigg, who commissioned it. The box pews are late 18th-century.

There is a fine series of medieval memorial brasses commemorating early owners of Felbrigg (see p.5) and wall monuments, including a modest stone tablet by the great woodcarver Grinling Gibbons for William Windham I (d.1689) and a grander bust on a sarcophagus by Joseph Nollekens for William Windham III (d.1810).

Right The nave of St Margaret's church

Below St Margaret's church in the open parkland

The Estate

The core of the Felbrigg estate predates the Domesday Book (1086) and was gradually expanded during the medieval period by a mixture of shrewd purchase and brute force. Among the estates added to Felbrigg were Sustead and Beeston Priory. By careful management in the late 17th century, William Windham I, and later his widow Katherine, were able to extract a profit from many of their farms by taking them in hand. Their achievement was all the more remarkable because this was a period of poor returns from agriculture. A century later William Windham III's steward Nathaniel Kent enclosed much of the common land, effectively dispossessing the villagers of their grazing rights. His other efforts as an improving agent were less contentious. Kent publicised his achievements in *A General View of the Agriculture of Norfolk* (1796), which had already been endorsed by William Marshall in his *Rural Economy of Norfolk* (1787).

The estate reached its highpoint during the era of William Howe Windham in the early 1840s, when it comprised over 10,000 acres. He erected many new farm buildings and estate cottages, which were carefully identified by stone tablets. He also commissioned the neo-Jacobean Cromer Lodges at the main entrance to the estate in 1841 from J.C. and G. Buckler. The estate went rapidly downhill after the abolition of the Corn Laws in 1846 and the disastrous era of 'Mad' Windham, when much of the estate was mortgaged. What little remained was sold to John Ketton in 1863. The Ketton-Cremers did their best to repair the gaps, but when the estate came to the National Trust in 1969, its acreage comprised only a fifth of what it had been in 1854.

Above The Windham coat of arms on the East Lodge

Top The Cromer Lodges in the 19th century

Above Frederick Ward, head keeper on the Felbrigg estate in the early 1900s

Wildlife

Below A Daubenton's bat hunting insects over water

Felbrigg's diverse habitats have something to offer the nature lover at every season. At dusk pipistrelle and Daubenton's bats circle the lake on the lookout for insects. Felbrigg supports eight species of bat in all, four of which hibernate in the ice house. Barn and Little Owls glide silently over the open fields hunting their prey.

The pastures attract such traditional farmland birds as song thrush, skylarks, linnets and yellowhammers, while the woodlands are the domain of the Great Spotted and Green Woodpeckers, which are more often to be heard than seen. Flocks of Bramblings feast on a rich diet of beechmast (the fruit of the beech tree) in the autumn. Fallen trees are usually left to rot where they lie, as they provide a welcome habitat for a wide variety of insects and fungi. Dragonflies hawking around the lake include red-veined darter and small red-eyed damselfly.

Felbrigg in spring

'Jackdaws chatter as they make their nests in the hollow beeches. Cock pheasants, spectacular in their mating plumage, crow and drum their wings. In the trees near the church a pair of kestrels is sure to breed, and occasionally I hear their shrill mewing note. Late in April the cuckoos come. But the dominant note, always and inescapably, is the crying of the plovers.'

R.W. Ketton-Cremer